MEERKATS

Clara Reade

PowerKiDS press
New York

For the Cox twins

Published in 2013 by The Rosen Publishing Group, Inc.
29 East 21st Street, New York, NY 10010

Copyright © 2013 by The Rosen Publishing Group, Inc.

All rights reserved. No part of this book may be reproduced in any form without permission in writing from the publisher, except by a reviewer.

First Edition

Editor: Amelie von Zumbusch
Book Design: Greg Tucker

Photo Credits: Cover, pp. 5, 7, 9, 11, 13, 15, 17, 21, 23, 24 (upper-left), 24 (upper-right) Shutterstock.com; p. 19 David W. Macdonald/Oxford Scientific/Getty Images.

Library of Congress Cataloging-in-Publication Data

Reade, Clara.
 Meerkats / by Clara Reade. — 1st ed.
  p. cm. — (Powerkids readers: safari animals)
 Includes index.
 ISBN 978-1-4488-7394-4 (library binding) — ISBN 978-1-4488-7474-3 (pbk.) — ISBN 978-1-4488-7547-4 (6-pack)
 1. Meerkat—Juvenile literature. I. Title.
 QL737.C235R43 2013
 599.74'2—dc23

2011049396

Manufactured in the United States of America

CPSIA Compliance Information: Batch #CS12PK: For Further Information contact Rosen Publishing, New York, New York at 1-800-237-9932

CONTENTS

Meerkats at Home	4
Meerkat Mobs	10
Pups	22
Words to Know	24
Index	24
Websites	24

Meerkats live in the ground.

5

They live in Africa.

They lie in the sun to warm up.

A group of meerkats is
a **mob**.

Meerkats work together.

When some look for enemies, others find food.

Insects are their main food.

They eat **scorpions**, too!

Meerkats find their food
by smell.

Babies are called **pups**.

WORDS TO KNOW

mob

pups

scorpion

INDEX

F
food, 14, 16, 20

G
ground, 4
group, 10

P
pups, 22

S
scorpions, 18
sun, 8

WEBSITES

Due to the changing nature of Internet links, PowerKids Press has developed an online list of websites related to the subject of this book. This site is updated regularly. Please use this link to access the list:
www.powerkidslinks.com/pkrs/meer/